# The Road to Recovery is Paved with Dog Treats!

### Patricia A. Brill, PhD

Illustrated by Curt Walstead

This book is dedicated to Dr. Larry Flemming
of Marina Bay Animal Hospital and Dr. Blaine Burkert
of Bay Area Veterinary Surgical Group, L.L.P.
Their hard work, compassion and dedication are
critical in ensuring the very best care for Turbo
as well as well as hundreds of other dogs and cats.

Hello All—

The story I am about to tell you is about what happens to dogs and cats when they have to have surgery. I consider myself an expert because so far I have had three surgeries to remove some cancerous moles from my legs, back, and stomach, and another surgery to repair a ligament in my knee. After my first surgery, the technicians called me *Frankendog!*

Although my person called Dr. Pat worried throughout every surgery, I was not afraid. I made it a point to reassure all the other dogs and cats that everything would be okay. It was my goal to be a friend to them and help them relax and feel happy and safe, but sometimes they were still scared.

I hope this book will help you understand what happens when your pet has surgery, and will relieve some of your worries.

Love,

Turbo

"ARRROOOOO!"

Startled by the howl, Turbo jumped and hit his head on the top of his cage. He looked around, and in the cage next to him was a small dog huddled in the corner.

"What's wrong?" inquired Turbo.
"I'm scared," cried Murphy. "I have to have surgery tomorrow. I've never had surgery before."

"Why do you have to have surgery?" Turbo asked.

"Because I accidently swallowed some of my person's items. Usually when I am left home alone, I tend to chew on something that has his scent. That helps me not to feel so lonely. But today I swallowed them. When my person came home, he found me lying on the floor moaning and groaning. So he immediately brought me to see the Vet called Dr. Thornburg. She took an x-ray of my stomach."

"What did she find?" asked Turbo.
"Just a sock, a pair of underwear, and a guitar pick," replied Murphy.

"Guitar pick!" exclaimed Turbo.
"What can I say," said Murphy. "My person likes to play the blues."

"Turbo, would you please explain to me what will happen when Dr. Thornburg operates on me?"

"Sure," said Turbo. "This is how it will work. Right before your surgery the Nurse called Lisa will place you on a shiny cold bed and wheel you into the operating room. But don't worry," assured Turbo, "the bed isn't as cold as it looks." Murphy shivered.

"Then Doctor Thornburg will put on clean scrubs and a mask. She will wash her hands and lower arms. Then once you are in the operating room they will give you anesthesia to help you fall asleep for a little while. That way you won't feel any pain when they make an incision to remove the items you swallowed."

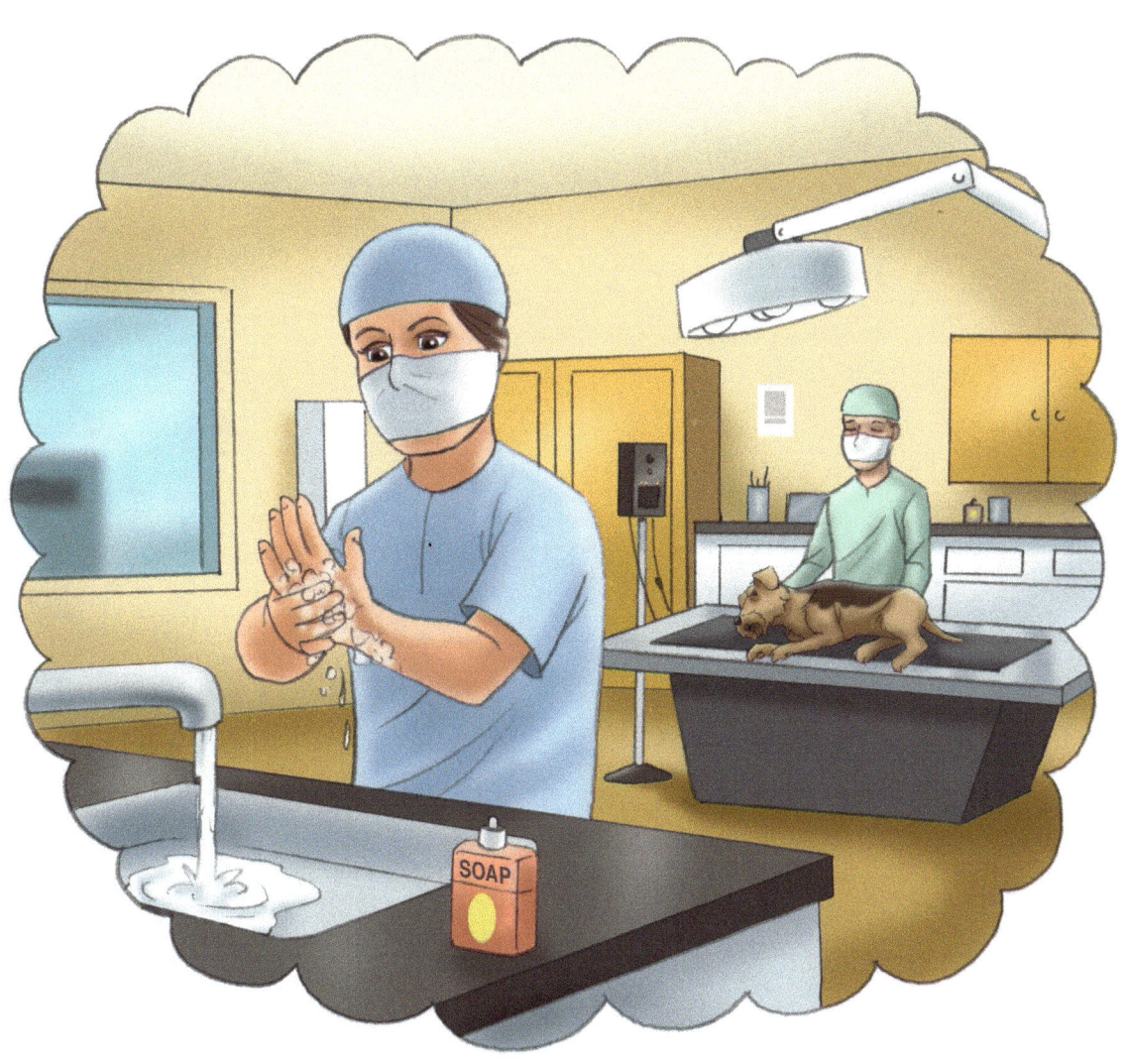

"Put me to sleep!" yelped Murphy. "What if I don't wake up? Or what if I wake up and no one is there? What if . . ."

"Slow down," shouted a cat from the other side of the room. "You worry too much!"

Murphy glared at the cat. "Why are you here and what is that silly cone doing around your head?"

"Well if you must know," admitted the cat, "one morning I ate too much cat nip and decided I could fly. So I climbed to the top of the counter; took a running leap; and crashed to the floor breaking my leg. Talk about being embarrassed. I had to have surgery to repair my leg. And for your information, the cone is necessary to prevent me from licking my stitches and getting them infected."

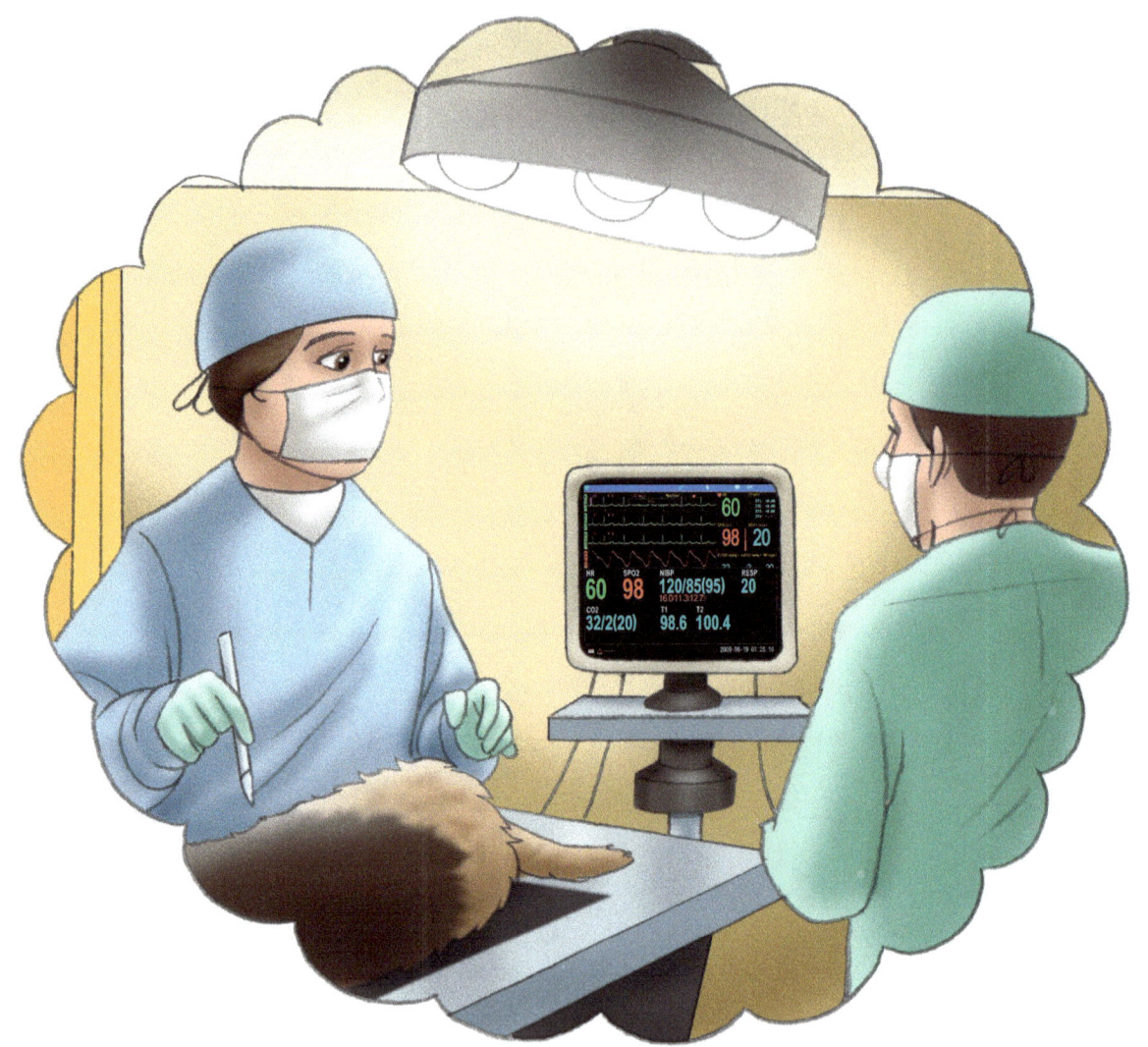

Turbo glanced at the cat and continued. "During your surgery Murphy, you will be monitored frequently with a tool that records your heart rate, blood pressure, and oxygen levels to make sure you are safe. Once the surgery is over, Dr. Thornburg will close the incision."

"How many surgeries have you had?" asked Murphy.

"So far I have had three surgeries to remove some cancerous moles from my legs, back, and stomach. After my first surgery, they called me Frankendog! I was scared, but the Nurse called Lisa was always with me. She even brought me treats!"

"My fourth surgery was to repair a torn ligament in my knee. My Vet called Dr. Larry told me I had to stay calm for two weeks which meant no running, jumping, spinning, or playing with my brother and sisters. So to prevent re-injuring my knee I had to stay here. During that time I watched the vets perform surgery on several dogs and cats."

"How long do surgeries last?" asked Murphy.

"It depends on the type of surgery," said Turbo. "Your surgery may only take an hour, unless they find more items in your stomach. But more complicated surgeries, like the cat with the broken leg, took several hours."

"Will my incision hurt after my surgery?" whined Murphy.

"You may feel some pain or discomfort for a few days after your surgery," replied Turbo, "but Dr. Thornburg will give you some pills to make the pain go away."

"What if I wake up and no one is there?" whimpered Murphy.

"Don't worry," reassured Turbo. "I'll be right here when you wake up, as well as the Nurse called Lisa. The first thing you will see is her smiling face. She loves animals, almost as much as I love treats!"

Murphy sighed, "Is that all you think about?"

Turbo continued, "Once you are in recovery, they will place a cone around your head, just like the cat was wearing, to prevent you from licking or chewing your stitches. They call it the cone of shame. You will look silly, but the cone will help prevent infection."

"Why does Dr. Thornburg want me to stay overnight? Why can't I just go home after my surgery?" asked Murphy.

"Because Dr. Thornburg cares about you and wants you to be well enough before you go home. She just wants you to wait a day or two before it is safe for you to run and jump and spin and play."

"Will I have to have surgery again?" asked Murphy.

"Not unless you swallow more of your person's items," said Turbo. "Let me give you some advice. Next time you are missing your person, strum his guitar or sleep on his pillow."

"How long does it take to recover from a surgery?" Murphy asked.

"For your type of surgery, it should only take a couple of days. Other types of surgeries, like the cat with the broken leg will take longer to recover."

"What if I can't eat after my surgery?" asked Murphy.

Turbo giggled. "I don't know about that. I've never had that problem. After my surgeries I always tried to wake up early just to get a treat from the Nurse called Lisa."

"Treats again? Oh Turbo you worry me."

The Nurse called Lisa came to get Murphy to take him to surgery. "Don't worry," reassured Turbo, "everything will be okay. I'll be right here when you get back."

Turbo waited patiently until Murphy returned.

"Hi Turbo," whispered Murphy. "Thanks for waiting for me."

"Of course!" said Turbo. "That's what friends are for. So how did your surgery go?"

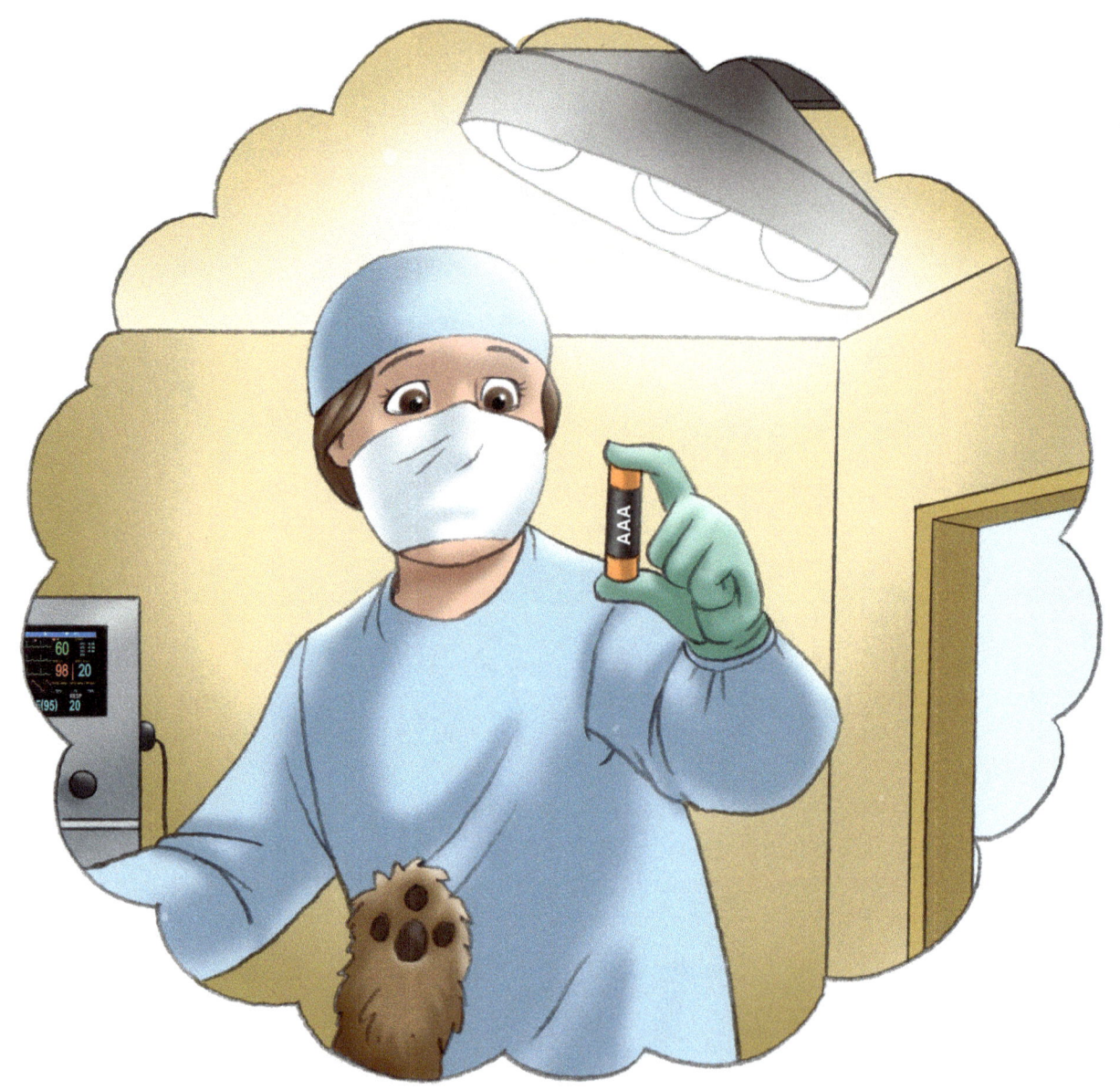

Murphy replied, "The vet called Dr. Thornburg said it was a success. However, in addition to removing a sock, a pair of underwear, and a guitar pick, she also removed a AAA battery."

The following morning Murphy was allowed to go home.
"See You!" yelled Turbo. "Later!" snarled the cat.
"BarK! BarK! BarK! BarK! BarK!" sang all the other dogs.

*The Road to Recovery is Paved with Dog Treats*

© 2015 by Patricia A. Brill

Published by Functional Fitness L.L.C.

All rights reserved. No part of this book may be reproduced, stored, or transmitted by any mean (paperback)s--whether auditory, graphic, mechanical, or electronic—without written permission of the author, except for the inclusion of brief quotes in critical articles and reviews. Send inquiries to info@dogtalescollection.com.

ISBN: 978-0-9815551-8-8 (paperback)

Printed in America

Illustrated by Curt Walstead

Book design by DesignForBooks.com